Enter the Chrysanthemum

Caitlin Press Inc.
8100 Alderwood Road, Halfmoon Bay, BC, V0N 1Y1
www.caitlin-press.com

Cover design by David Drummond.
Text design by the house.
Printed in Canada

Caitlin Press Inc. acknowledges financial support from the Government of Canada through the Book Publishing Industry Development Program and the Canada Council for the Arts, and from the Province of British Columbia through the British Columbia Arts Council and the Book Publisher's Tax Credit.

**Canada Council
for the Arts**

**Conseil des Arts
du Canada**

BRITISH COLUMBIA
ARTS COUNCIL

Library and Archives Canada Cataloguing in Publication

Lam, Fiona Tinwei, 1964–
    Enter the chrysanthemum / Fiona Tinwei Lam.

Poems.

ISBN 978-1-894759-32-8

    I. Title.

PS8573.A38383E58 2009   C811'.6   C2009-900514-X

Enter the Chrysanthemum

Poems by

Fiona Tinwei Lam

Caitlin Press

For my parents and my son.

Contents

Four

One

There is having by having
and having by remembering.
—Linda Gregg, "Winning"

Chrysanthemum

Rolls of rice paper in the corner,
jars of soft-haired brushes,
elegant cakes of watercolour,
black inkstone at the centre.

My mother held the brush vertically,
never slant, arm and fingers poised,
distilling bird or breeze into
diligent rows of single characters.

Hours rippled. Years of practice urged
the true strokes forth—stiff bamboo
now waving in white air, cautious lines
now ribboning silk folds of a woman's gown.

My favourite of her paintings
was of chrysanthemums. They began
as five arcs of ink, long breaths in the emptiness
alluding to stem and blossom. Then,

from the finest brush, the outline of each petal.
Flesh flowed from the fuller one, tipped
with yellow or lavender, until every crown
bloomed amid the throng of leaves.

If only I had been paper,
a delicate, upturned face stroked
with such precise tenderness.

Before Breakfast

Before breakfast, I'd hear him
in the bathroom behind the laundry room
at the far side of the house.
The raspy hum of his electric shaver
as he mowed slow, even rows down
cheekbone, jaw and neck. I'd wander over
to watch him see himself
in the small mirror. With a comb, he'd draw
the clear cream through the licorice
of his hair, pat it down in place,
a glossy mantle over the high dome
of his head. He'd knot his tie
as if joining head to body
and suddenly become the father
I knew best, the smooth calm gleam
of ironed shirt, wool suit, black shoes
readied to leave us.

We rarely talked or touched.
But each night, as ordered,
I'd tiptoe up, he'd lean his six feet down,
and my lips would feel
the remnant of his day's smoothness
giving way to night's faint bristle.

Waiting

I'll be back soon, my dad would say
putting on his doctor's face
before doing his rounds.

I'd sit in the station wagon
in the hospital parking lot, draw a crowd
of circle-faces on the window,
my fingertips wet and grey like old bandages,
or sing choruses from Beatles' songs—
"Let It Be," "All You Need Is Love"—
then surrender to blankness
fractured by shoe-scrapes and key-jangles.
Slouched in my seat, I wanted to be
impermeable as brick walls, blinded windows.

I imagined him striding down the hall
in his white coat, prince/priest.
Babies mewling in glass cages.
Children inert as dolls,
tubes worming from their arms.
Cool balm of his hands
upon their fevers, contusions.
Duets of lung and heart funnelled
through the flat bell of his stethoscope.
Parents were a backdrop, faces
bruised with worry.

I could have walked home
if I'd known the direction.
Instead, I'd push the car door ajar,
dangle my feet outside to measure
the world against my shoes, then
seal myself in with a slam,
proving my love until he returned
to drive us away to someplace else
where I'd wait once again.

Home

When I was three and crossed my eyes, tendriled creatures
floated up from my room's patterned carpet,
crowding my room, whirling. I hid behind the door
and heard my mother storming around my father.
Head bent, he seemed to be listening
to the furniture, which somehow made him weep.

How I loved him then, my fellow hostage.
He sat the way I would sit, beneath her
brandished voice. The door creaked.
She found me curled and cramped on the floor.

No tapped greetings between walls for us. Just
mute dialogues with the inanimate
while she flailed at him, indecipherable
torrents of Cantonese punctuated
by pots and plates flung at linoleum.

After he died, she would retreat alone each year
to mourn his passing. All along, she'd been blinded,
one lost child crying out to another,
through his echoing cells, even the ones
that would betray him, that carried his death;
calling to the chambers of his flayed heart.

New Year's Eve

    Once a year, our mother dragged out the old Chinese cookbook with the cracked covers. We'd wash down the table with hot tea while she shoved hunks of cabbage through the grinder. When the white shreds were heaped in the blue bowl, she'd add minced meat, splash and spoon in the seasonings, blending them all with bare hands. Into another bowl, she'd scoop flour, pour water, mix them, and start massaging the paste into muscle. She'd tear off a wad, knead it down to a disk, roll it in flour, then crank it through the machine. Side by side, my sister and I would start cutting circles out of the long skin of dough, gathering the scraps to re-roll, re-cut, tossing a few lumps for our little brother to play with. At table's end, my mother would stuff the circles with filling, crimping the edges.

When the rows packed the trays, she'd move to the stove, to the bubbling pot, the pan spitting oil, to boil and fry. We'd wash up. Soon, she'd fish out the steaming pillows of dough, and slide out the crisp ones, glistening, from skillet to plate where they'd be devoured as fast as they landed. Each hot morsel dipped in sauce, barely chewed, swallowed. Then the second batch, throat to belly. The slightly slower third. Sated at last, we'd surrender, dazed at what we'd waited months for: real food—what came from her hands.

Family Doctor

Our mother would gripe *I need a wife,*
as she'd trudge through the door
shoulders bowed, eyes grim from a day's load
of patients, babies, bills. Silence clamped down
on our after-school voices: we'd gauge her face
for bad weather, minute shifts in the terrain
of muscle around mouth and eyes.
We'd tuck away consent forms, invitations,
and hunker down. Through supper, the quiet
would fill, swallow by swallow.

A few times she'd take us on house calls,
her Corolla inching up dim side streets on the hunt
for some feverish kid. Each of us would peer
past bushes, unlit porches for house numbers,
sailors navigating passage through fog.

Past midnight, the phone would jangle
our dreams. She'd leave to nap at the hospital,
burrowed beneath her coat, awaiting
a pre-dawn birth. All next day,
her blood ran brown from cheap coffee
downed between patients, bitter edges blunted
by tilts of sugar, pyramids of cream.

Other nights, sink jammed, fridge gaping,
she'd marshall us out to eat. We'd go
wherever we'd go, sit wordlessly and watch
our mother crumple, lay her head gently on the table,
close her eyes, fall through the world.

Origami

Crease, fold and turn,
crease, fold, and open.
Her surgeon's, dumpling-making,
dexterous hands would work the paper
rummaged from her purse:
a sampan from a lipstick ad,
a canoe from an envelope, and off
she'd march to kids fretting at a nearby table
to bestow her gifts.

From my place, I'd watch them
swish their boats around cups and plates
on formica seas, wishing again
for the cranes she once made us
with heads that bobbed when we pulled their tails—
how supper flew!

But I was mere spectator now,
too teenaged to be happy.
The paper gates to childhood
completely closed.

Weed Killer

Our mother gave us a sack of weed killer
the size of a toddler, and told us
to spread it on the front lawn.

My sister and I lugged it there.
A light cloud of white powder
drifted up to our nostrils
and down to our tongues, blooming sour
wherever it touched membrane.
We scooped the stuff out with teenaged zeal
as we dusted the lawn, checkerboard lines
mounded where the grass was thin.

We thought we were done,
but there was still half a sack left.
So we poured again,
more diligently, layering it thick
as it caked in our nails and our palms.
The lines dispersed into snowdrift
wafted by the breeze to our clothes and hair
to neighbourhood gardens, cars, open windows,
to people chatting or eating,
to birds, beyond birds.

We were proud farmers
over a crop we'd just saved.
Then our mother returned
to tell us we'd done it all wrong.

The soft sourness lingered for days
as we watched the lawn choke,
its yellowing skin shrivelling
into bald, numbed soil
that took years to recover.

That fine bitter powder bestowed by our mother,
scattered like ashes over our lives
to steep in blood and bind with tears
in the slow dark turn
of flesh and earth against breath.

Funeral March

At the centre of sound,
my mother splayed her fingers
over the piano's glossy teeth,
wrists weighed down. She hunched
over the great black body, clenched chords
staggering down the hall double *forté*.
Beneath bunkers of blankets and pillows,
we gritted our teeth.

Decades later, I lead her to the bench,
lift the lid with its pelt of dust
to play for her. My hands mutter
gloom up an incline of octaves.

She listens a moment.
Says she's heard it
but never played it—
something to do with funerals.

She takes over the keyboard
with fleet, easy hands:
a nursery rhyme,
ripples of the "Blue Danube,"
a last round of "Auld Lang Syne."

Return

Dressed in our cast-offs,
she'd greet us at the door
of the home we'd left behind.
Nothing new allowed in
except dollar store finds—
brass horse-head bookends, fox-hunting trivets.
Plastic bags full of plastic bags
hoarded and forgotten in the dining room.
The heat shut off in half the house,
the refrigerator stacked with atrophied
Chinese take out, our childhoods jammed
in downstairs drawers—Monopoly, Snakes and Ladders
minus the tokens, the dice. And that old box
in the furnace room, packed
with tangled extension cords, connecting
nothing to nothing.

Father's Day

This day at the cemetery,
small splashes of flowers
in the place of men.
I stand beside my mother,
her grandchild afloat within me.

My sister bends by my father's plaque,
arranging chrysanthemums, gerberas.
My brother tugs at overgrown grass,
crinkling cellophane
our only conversation.

We ready ourselves, then bow
three times in unison, hands clasped,
knots against the heart.

After, in the empty restaurant,
we prop ourselves around her
like sun-bleached photographs
of the vaguely familiar.
We pour her tea, count out her pills,
cast our little hooks of words
to try to snag what isn't there.

Back at her house of boxes and piles,
all things once rooted
now dangle mid-air.
Complicitous, we wander
into the brimming vacancy
of each room, picking through

a life disassembled and culled
to fit the neat, blank corners
of a nursing home.

My mother asks again
what day it is.
The answer brushes past,
vanishes.

Call

These days, every hour or less,
a phone call from my mother.

She flails and clutches at me through the line.
Help me. But I can't drag her out.

I say *it's alright, it's alright.*
But it's not and I can't
stop the dark as it pushes her in.

What's left of her memory,
a skim of debris
that disintegrates while she flounders.

Words have no arms.
I love you saves no one
and soon I'll cry too
from what's gouged away
beneath the soothe and the lull
of my voice.

I'll coax out a blanket of sleep
and tuck it around her,
make her forget the forgetting.

Until the numbers too begin drifting
just out of grasp. Just like the daughter
I will no longer be.

Dream

Three fetuses pulled out of my womb
too early, in error. I run to the faucet,
immerse them in buckets of water
where they float untethered,
spines furled around hearts encased
in almost-bone and almost-skin,

and run again, dangling ropes of flesh,
crying to you, my mother, the doctor,
to reverse what I've done, save
what is asphyxiating
second by seeping second.

You won't listen.
You lie in your room, curtains drawn,
surly and closed on your bed
the way you were years ago,
flattened by queues of sick families,
the house calls and stillbirths.

Too difficult you pronounce,
and turn away. Your face a pale pill
dissolving in the liquid night.

Two

day draws near
another one
do what you can.
    —Czeslaw Milosz, "On Angels"

Eleventh Avenue

Hand in hand, we hobbled out of the house
my first day back from hospital. Together alone,
with newly seamed aches—
you with your ripped knee,
me with a wrenched, emptied womb.

We steadied each other
as if we'd just arisen from disbelief
after a year of reeling through desire's tectonics.
First steps along scarred sidewalks
toward what we'd become.

This was our aisle, the only one
I would know with you.
Without trumpets or processional,
four blocks, fifteen minutes, witnessed
by maples waving their bud-flecked branches.

That February day, the cusp,
sky austere with dusk,
a light rain anointing us all.
We returned—a father, a mother
to our son.

Colic

You hold him. Hold him against your stained T-shirt.
At two months he still moans, writhes in his sleep.

breast bottle soother pacing swaddling swinging lullabies
chamomile gripe-water hugging rubbing pacing patting rocking

You've wobbled through weeks of this, ready to fall
through your stitches onto the floor or the street.

The experts advise what you already know.
No antidote. How can you sleep
when his sleep is agony?

And the baby's father, when he's there,
broods on the outskirts of love.

breast rocking pacing swaddling chamomile lullabies
pacing gripe-water rocking swinging singing pacing

You wait it out. All you can do—
keep vigil.

Milk

Small, sweaty cannibal.
At the pull of his call,
muscle and tendon liquefied.
The tiny machine of his mouth
nibbled and sucked the hours.

One night as he slept,
a hot boulder swelled
in my left breast, veins stiffly blue.
I lay shuddering on the bed.
I made myself rise,

found a candle. Lit it. Assembled
a needle from a hotel sewing kit,
alcohol, cotton, hot cloth.
Read and reread paragraphs
in a text on nursing.

I held the needle to the flame,
then foraged through the blockage,
squeezed the swelling down,
until a delicate arc of white
sprayed across the bed.

Even now, he wants it,
gropes through my shirt
to anchor his comfort
in the sweet white blood
of all I can be.

Naming

My child pulls his hand from mine,
becomes an urgent arrow aimed
at the universe.

Discovery gleams into utterance:
Moon! He claims the sliver of deep light
for himself and for me.

Moon! His sigh, silvery and rich,
as we return to our orbits,
vibrating glory.

Beach

Foraging for treasure in summer's ruins:
cigarette butts, broken shells, a blackened match.
Grim-faced, you won't look up
at gulls, planes. Even the children,
their siege of shrieks.

The waves make you cry,
their ceaseless crashing,
the murky sluice of water, thick
with matted seaweed,
yellow foam.

Castles carefully tipped out
of plastic buckets, grainy cakes adorned
with twigs and pebbles—
you topple them all,
trudge away.

During the car ride home,
the look you give me
is an old man's relief.
At last we've left
the roar of the world.

Ablution

A two day deluge.
The snow family I made—
hats, gloves, carrot noses, strewn
in shrinking grey mush.
The proud pathways shovelled out
for nothing. Everything
running in the gutters.

After weeks' worth of wrestling him
into his stroller, tantrums in shop aisles,
strained lullabies, night terrors,
chairs heaped with laundry,
I at last put him down
for the nap we both need,
my brain a slow smoulder.

Ten minutes later, he shifts
in his sheets, kicking off blankets, rising
while I sink.

Rain, scour my spirit.
Cleanse this day of its little fists.

Glass

A treacherous brown sea spread out on the floor,
a full litre of syrup studded with splintered glass.
I was stranded with bare feet in a corner
like a civilian in a minefield. My toddler
scurried towards the kitchen, whimpering
while I scooped up sticky shards. *Danger! You'll get hurt!*
His little craving body wavered. *Stay away!*
On the brink, he teetered forward
and everything crashed inside me.
I ran through the glass, grabbed him, blasting,
blaming until my shouting went beyond sound.

Suddenly my son's face became mine as a child, frozen
before the contortions of my mother's fury.
My own face stiffened into its inheritance,
the familiar mask that was my mother's,
raising three children alone, and my grandmother's,
widowed with nine kids during the war,
and her mother's—generations of unmothered women
bereaved, laden with family, raging,
back and further back, until they were specks
within the eye of an eye.

My son clung to me in terror—
all those mothers shrieking through my skin.
As he sobbed, I soothed him, carried him
to a chair, glass grinding into every step. Later,
washed and bandaged my feet, forgiving
my mother the small crimes I'd tallied against her,
childhood trails of blood wiped clear.

Park

The mother closes her eyes
so her eyelids can fall
even if the rest of her can't.

She leans against the stroller,
pushing a strapped-in toddler
across blasts of car exhaust.

They arrive finally
at the bounded universe of sand and grass,
children spinning and clambering
within pockets of glee,
thuds and skids of balls and boards,
parental pleas muted by summer air.

She places him in the sandbox.
Crouched on the sidelines
under a flicker of shade,
she pretends to monitor
the progress of his front-end loader.

But he just wants to run
to the expanse of green, through to
openness.
He reaches up at a helicopter,
a small unity of bone, muscle and breath
aching for flight.

She gathers what is left of herself
to mark movement through the sky,
her weary loving face
on the perimeter of joy.

Lost

For Alex Pierce

I look up. Across the water park, a woman
staggers as if out of a surrealist painting,
her child lost in the blur of
running and splashing,
her mouth a twisted pit,
repeated calls drowned out.

The water turned off, everyone ordered to sit.
Staff range through the park
while I start remembering—pink scraps
of membrane floating out from my body,
adrift in the bath. That night in Tofino,
how I fled the tub, daubing myself,
every stain an omen.
Until morning, I curled my limbs around you,
sealing in the twelve weeks of your life.
The clinic doctor searched in vain for your heartbeat,
all meaning reduced—to seeing you
twirl and flip again on the screen.
Next day, I returned to the city.
Through the Doppler, your heart's tiny drum—
you were back!
Re-emerging like the boy tucked away
in the park, astonished
to find he'd been lost.

How his mother holds him
as she walks through the holiday of water,
the way I held you, every cell
cupped within my body's fierce cradle.

Nursing Home

My son runs to hug her.
She doesn't know his name,
asks about my other children,
ones I've never had.

When she tries to grab his arm,
he prances past dazed residents
arranged like potted plants around
a yammering TV.
He scampers through the corridors,
turns the corner—she wonders
if he's been kidnapped.

But in her room,
they each take a harmonica.
and commence a conversation
of blasted notes and chords, loud
and louder with each turn.
He laughs. In the dissonance,
the walls collapse
before they rise again.

After the Party

We leave laden with loot from the party—
chocolate coins, stickers, dollar store toys.
The little blue man with the parachute
won't float, only plummet, so I promise
to fix it when we get home. A birthday
balloon tied to my purse strap bobs and glows,
a small orange shadow against our dark
silhouettes. Plodding, criss-crossing the streets,
I carry him on my back, hunched over
and sweating from his leggy weight. We reach
Cambie street, its long wound of construction—
loaders, cranes, and trucks paralyzed mid-roar,
squashed traffic cones, crumbled road, stacks of pipe.

Four blocks ahead, shady oaks and maples,
the crisp cracks of balls on bats. Children swoop
themselves into a breeze. An ice-cream truck
tinkles. My son wriggles free, my purse drops.
The balloon gives us the slip, lifting past
roofs and treetops to the beckoning blue.

Cinderella Retires

Today, in the rain, I am almost beautiful.
But there's no prince to see it.
Somehow this morning without my knowing,
my body scraped together the glints
of leftover brilliance
and I can shimmer again. I had days
of ripeness, but now
just surprise flickerings.

The day fades, as the green, red, then yellow
fade from the trees. There's still
a bit of silk in my skin,
a round heat to my lips. My breasts
are not utterly dejected. Yet

this will soon seep away. Brittle leaves
crumble into earth. Attempts at radiance,
seen or unseen, done.

Shower

Those mornings we're together, the three of us
stand in a spray of soft diamonds—sunlight
through glass, and everything sparkling.
You hold our son high in your arms
while I lather him up. Our little otter,
he's as sleek and slick as when he slid
from my womb. Then I lather you,
foot to thigh, chest to back—the heft and sinew
of what I have loved. You and he both
turn in the warm rain, my universe
of king and prince rinsed to a glisten.
When you soap my skin, I live,
become brief silk in your hands, as luscious
as when your desire flowed. Only water
will love me when you are gone.

House

A day for the groceries,
a day for the dough,
a day to roll, cut, bake and cool,
a day to ice the sides, pattern the candies.
The last day to assemble the house
with a plugged-up pastry tube.

My son watched the candies tumble.
No matter how I iced it or propped it up,
the roof slid down. Then broke—
that Christmas and New Year's,
my son's father with a new woman.

This year, the house is smaller.
My son makes a gingerbread self,
a dad, a mom—all burnt.
We eat them, cut new ones
from the spare roof, and bake again,
his father and I lying chastely on the sheet.

When it's time to assemble it,
I consult my son. He tells me
the gingerbread boy wants to play
with the other gingerbread kids,
but later decides the son will stay
by the house with his mother.

The father floats about uncertainly
until we place him by the door,
one hand resting on the boy's head.
Cemented in their places,
the father and mother will only
hold hands through their son.

Three

When we belong to the world
we become what we are.
—Anne Stevenson,
"Poem for a Daughter"

Rapunzel

I want to say *Make love to me*
but instead, I mention the weather—
after weeks of damp, the air
is as mild as spring's, the skies
swept clear of cloud.
I'm restless, tired of my tower
of virtue, this higher ground.

I want to say *Climb up*.
These nights alone,
I've made my hands yours,
the gaze of your palms
upon the gaze of my flesh.
You've opened me. I'm here,
waiting. Enter
what I've let no man enter:
Let us become
first woman, first man
in the garden of our limbs.
I'm eager for your body's salt.
My hair flows down.

Real

It's a disorder of sorts,
not just about mattresses.
Sometimes it's the sheets or pillows.
More often, the man.

Many a sleepless night,
I've gritted my teeth
while he scrapes his bristle
along my breasts and thighs.

Don't bother counting my scars
from hangnailed caresses.
Crowned by their mothers,
these "princes" are nothing but brutes.

I'm tired of tests, hidden peas.
Yet still I keep seeking shelter
in the one who can treasure
what's real, not plunder it.

Mermaid

My father and sisters weeping from shore,
my grandmother mourning in our coral home,
my splendid tail, my lyric tongue—all severed,
the price for these cursed legs.

How my smile hid the stab of each step
while I danced for you and your friends.
You never looked at the bloody stub
where the witch sundered my tongue.

You've forgotten how we rode together,
climbed mountains, watched clouds
stream beneath us like white-flecked water.
The way I burned outside your door.

When I saw her pearls pooled on your dresser,
her stiletto heels beside your bed, I knew
defeat, more exquisitely precise
than the thousand blades through my feet.

Your bride is ravishing, meant for you
as I was meant for no one.
My blue shadow, a scar
beneath the sinking red sun.

Christmas Eve Afternoon

Screw you, said the girl, glaring,
as she lurched into the bus seat I'd already claimed,
her scowl lunging down the aisle,

like the one from the antique vendor
who tore up the fifty dollar invoice for the three-inch tin robot
I thought was five bucks.

Elusive gifts. Shuttered shops.
Winter wind seeping through my coat's every seam.
My arms bereft without my son.

The movie was no distraction—
the heroine drowns, the hero consumed by septicemia—
the true price of three and a half minutes of love.

Three minutes, three months, three years—
whatever fragment was given, little persists,
as doors smack shut from stop to stop.

Mother

Smiling, almost alive, it marches
blank-eyed through the child's day,
buying mangoes, making jam,
booking play-dates, ensuring
the child has fresh underwear
and organic milk with meals.

Uniformed in flat shoes,
a thick smear of lipstick,
an outline of kohl, and a large sack
packed for every contingency—
heat wave, famine, storm, diarrhea.
Worst of all, boredom.

Sometimes the child isn't fooled.
He gnaws and kicks at it
to bring it back to the life
it barely lived before.
For he's hungry for something
it cannot offer.

When the child's away,
the switch flicks
off. It halts. Folds
itself into something very flat,
unites with the couch, mattress,
floor.

Jack's Mom

Boys. You just can't trust them.
Twelve days of shuddering chills and fever
locked me to this bed, otherwise
I would have taken our cow myself
to market. Don't get me wrong.
I love my silly son.
But I can't feed either of us
on five beans.

Crops failed, milk dried up.
Selling the beast was the last resort.
The trickster who took our cow
must be cackling over prime rib.

Last year it was magic potatoes.
Now it's magic beans.
What's next, rutabaga?
I pelted those blighted pods out the window.
Of course, now he's out there
hoeing and digging the winter soil
through his hunger and mine
as if his treasures will grow to the skies.

What can I say?
The boy has planted and watered
so many schemes.

Tonight, supperless, he will dream
the lottery of the luckless—
man-eating ogres, castles,

hens with golden eggs, a golden harp,
always those bags of gold.
A feast of riches erased by dawn.

Sleep, my fatherless one,
now you've swapped our lives away.
Climb your green ladders to the clouds.

Kite

He runs into the wind—
the kite rises. Swerves
against it—the kite dives.
Soon, the park is
festooned with colour:
streamers, planes, butterflies.
He runs on amid zigzags
of sprinting children,
dragging it along the battered grass
until moribund bird
becomes stubborn dog.
For a few metres, it whoops up
like a miracle, then
plummets. We try again.

A year ago, buffeted by wind,
he stood on a mound of sand and logs
by the beach. How he brimmed
sky and sunlight, first kite
soaring.

How I want that back.
Despite my warnings, he runs
between two gnarled trees,
wind behind him. The kite
sags, then snags.
I sigh, lecture, berate,
tug the kite one way, then the other,

finally break the string,
tangling both of us up
in that twisted, blunted tree.

He crouches pondside,
all jubilance flatlined.
One more time, I say.
He won't hear me.
My son and I, grounded
beneath vacant skies.

Snowman

Everyone praises my son
for the snowman on our front lawn:
porkpie hat, pebble smile,
the raised twig eyebrows slightly amused.

Silent, my son looks away.
How he laboured, rolling those balls
of snow around the lawn. Finally,
he enlisted my help. I stacked them,
brushed off the soil and leaves,
rounded off the corners, packed
the fault lines, fussed and shaped
to sculpt a face, adorn the head.
I offered him the eyes—
he shoved in the stones
and left. He was building
a mound he called a stage,
fifteen feet away. Room for one.

Two years ago, a wooden train set.
I spent an hour laying track
to form criss-crossed loops on the coffee table.
Anything he'd try to lay down
I dismantled, pleading for patience.
When I was done, he'd lost
interest. For weeks, that track lay there,
a masterpiece of devotion.
My son approached it once,
unsmiling, to connect a snaking line

of engines, cars, cabooses that derailed
on a corner going up a bridge.
He cried. I rushed over
with solace, advice. Only
when it crumbled away
could he create again,
without me.

At the Fundraiser

The blonde mother in the leather jacket
ensconced on a bench, mutters
a sour litany to the mother beside her,
their tired eyes trailing.
Her seven-year-old whines, waving
a balloon. The mother turns away.
The balloon keeps flapping.
That's enough, she says, strung taut.
The girl can't hear the warning,
or perhaps she does. She jumps up and down
as if to trample her mother's words,
tries to jump onto her lap.
No. Go play!
A push and swat.

The girl twirls away,
but returns to bop the balloon
in her mother's face as if to crack a shell—
the woman half-stands, grabs
the balloon as if it were her child's head,
her other hand a vise on her child's wrist.
Stop it! she hisses. *Go. Away.*
The spell works. The child dissolves—
erased.

Moon Goddess

I miss heaven. These mortals are dolts,
as burdened as their pack mules,
parched fields, snivelling infants.
I prefer the palaces, faint but constant music,
my swirling robes.

My husband, Hou Yi, shot down nine
of ten brutish suns to end the great drought.
Nine magic arrows from his celestial bow—
of course my idea. Yet he hid the reward:
glowing pills to live forever.

I hunted the house for their glimmer,
found them and swallowed fate.
Like a silk kite, I rose through the clouds.
His arrows whizzed past me.
So much for true love.

But heaven's gates slammed shut against thieves.
So into the moon with me,
a jade rabbit for company. How it thumps
and pounds through the days
with its mortar and pestle,

making more pills for no one
as we circle the earth. Now Hou Yi misses me.
Nothing like absence. On a full moon,
he's allowed a conjugal visit, but
I have such a headache.

Weddings

The bride's float plane
circled the crowd, a coy bird, before landing
at the shore of smiles and tears.
A measured glide to the groom, then
the joining. Feasting, dancing
amid candles and wine.
A month later, she left.

At another wedding years ago
a red hang-glider dove down
through the sky like an omen
into the orchard, into trees laden
with apples and plums,
disrupting the rabbi and vows.
Three children later, she too
parachuted out—no explanation.

My albums cluttered with the witnessing
of naive expectation in all its finery,
the rifts sheathed in satin, a sheen
of cosmetic bliss. Half the couples
now divided, main characters
hived off.

The petty wrongs accumulate
like hair in the drain. Bodies unravel,
too soon shapeless as the days, sacks
amassing daily sorrows until
at last it spills out—
what we didn't get, who failed us,
what seemed permanent, altered.
I didn't see it coming!
It was over long ago.

Scheherazade

Each day, a virgin.
Along streets, black wave upon black wave.
Sisterless, daughterless, this city
made graveyard by a cuckholded king
and his three-year tantrum of death.

I offered myself, took my place at his bed.
Before sunrise, I'd spun my silk threads
gleaned from the ancients—histories, fables
gathered for years. First one, then another,
tales within tales of fishermen, slaves,
sultans and sailors, a tapestry
woven of virtue and valour.
Night by long night, through
a thousand and one shimmering dawns
and the three heirs I bore him,
I built a true king.

Listen, my sisters. Words
can be spells. Satisfy,
do not sate. Always make of a man
the story he must become. Become yourself
a story, woven into his,
more intricate than a heart.

The Philistines

The Goliaths forever at war with the Davids,
uncultured brutes fighting to seize
what had been promised by God
to others. Didn't they know a promise is a promise?

My son asks,
Is their country still there?
What happened to them?

How do I explain history—
Shiites and Sunnis, Irish and Catholic,
Palestinians and Jews vying for a country?
No television sitcom, no video game
of bad guys and good guys, sparring
hockey teams vying for the cup.

But he's right to ask. Everyone marvels
at the marble statue of the beautiful victor.
Where's the statue of the vanquished,
those utterly wiped off the map—shards
in that slice of four-thousand-year-old
mud and broken pottery?

Water Park

A slide gushes children down to earth.
Parents sprinkled on the outskirts,
camped on beach towels on the grass,
desultory sentinels.

Yesterday, six Canadian soldiers
rode upon a gravel road near Kandahar
to their deaths. Sixty maimed.
Gouged lives bleeding into a pocked earth.
Parents, children, grandparents

far away from our splashes and delighted shrieks.
Nothing balanced on the scale.
Suffering, pleasure meted out
indifferently. This cold clear rain
under the bluest sky.

Playground

My son turns on the television,
wanting cartoons. Too late,
I sprint for the remote.
Scenes flash of bloody bundles—remains
of women, children lined up for a death count,
wailing family members. An ambush
of a home in an Iraqi town by American Marines—
at least twenty-four dead. My son tugs at my arm,
Who will make them come alive again?
They are dead, I explain, for good.
Why did they kill them? Is the war here?
No distance between him and the screen,
us and the world.

Since he was born, I can't turn on the news.
I leave the paper face down.

But there he is now, behind the trees
with the other boys. *Bam, bam!*
they shout, blasting each other
with fingers and sticks, hurling
pine cone grenades. Nobody plays
the peacekeeper, limbless children, mothers
begging in the streets.

Stories

He wants clarity, simplicity.
Not jealous, fuming brothers
selling their sibling as a slave
who are later forgiven;
certainly not a Herculean hero
who kills his babies.

He wants safety from evil—
good guys who stay good,
bad guys trounced.
Family members who never
destroy each other.

Why did he do that? he asks
overhearing talk about a husband
who brought poisoned milkshakes
to his wife in hospital. He asks again
through the day, the week.

Do I shield him, or tell him about cruelty?
I want to teach my son about peace.
He wants to be every superhero
he's ever heard of.

Remembrance Day

In front of his sons, my grandfather
crumpled on the street under a rain of kicks
and blows by Japanese soldiers.
His wives and daughters poised
to smear their faces and bodies with shit,
their only shield against another Nanking.

Now, clips of Vimy Ridge on television,
trenches, tanks, marching,
explosions in sepia, black and white.
Scenes of bombers droning like oversized flies
above a recent kill. Cities on fire.
Each labels the other side devils
while scorching homes to hell.

Downtown, a ceremony—
the choir sings its youthful grief,
a crowd, umbrellas, light rain,
the bugle's clear line of yearning
calling out to what continues
in Kabul, Tehran, Guantanamo—
five years of accumulating
death. A vigil to wait out the worst
we can be to each other.

Walking

My mother won't look at me or speak.
Her face is as clenched as her fists
pounding the table for breakfast.
Her cardigan's splotched from the meal,
her hair greasy. She won't let them
steal the clothes off her back,
let alone drown her. She knows
what those sweet-voiced bullies are after.
And who am I anyway?

I press the elevator code.
We descend from the third floor
back down to earth. Then out
into late August sunshine, world
made true by light.

We make our slow escape
from the garden, turn the corner.
A minute later, a smile starts to flower.
Her face lucent with sun,
she shuffle-trots down the sidewalk.
A hand pats a bush, gestures up at a fir.
You see, you see, she mumbles
with what's left of a jigsaw of words.

We reach Oak Street where there are no oaks—
only traffic blasting up and down a city spine.
Her eyes widen. A bus surges past.
Whee! she cries. Hand in my hand
by this roaring, clattering river,
my mother looks at me at last
and shouts, *You see, you see?*

Four

Each man is a half-open door
leading to a room for everyone.
—Tomas Tranströmer,
"The Half-Finished Heaven"

Dawn

Sleep-starved for weeks, I fight it
as I fight consciousness. Through the window,
light whispers. I hide my face.
It nudges. I turn my back.
It insists. I cry, relinquish myself
to another day's griefs.
Cocooned in a duvet, I sit at the shore
to meet whatever comes.

A gilding. A slow soak of radiance
at the crux. Father falling,
mother rising. My mother's turn
to die and rise.

He awaits her coming, as I awaited her
death in the hospital, her nine-hour marathon.
At the end of the long striving,
the blood's tributaries ebbed.
My hands became a child's,
absorbing solace from her warmth
before it fled. A gasp, a pause, release.
Gasp, pause, release. Silence.
Silence without.

The sun's slow glide
over the island toward the world.
Everything gives way at the melting point.
Sorrow begets joy begets sorrow.

The Bell

You want to be rung,
every cell rinsed with sound.
To be seized from doubt,
pulled ruthlessly into the world
your words have ached for.

Gleaming autumn light
through windows. Unequivocal
blue through gold-flecked maples.
Breathe, taste, hear, know
purpose. Make this city shimmer
or shudder. Joy or crisis—
each down the same spine.

Rainbow

He draws spiky red suns with sunglasses
surrounded by orange stars, clouds
with fat rain tears. Once, a rainbow
above the flight of round green birds.

Today, I open the back door
and urge him to my side to see
the great curving ribbons suspended above us
before they melt into sky.

We stand underneath
for a few glowing moments,
knowing colour
from the inside out.

Cup

For Susan Olding

Baked and glazed
to a sheen—a cup
to hold twilight.
It travelled across cities, nestled
in tissue, shielded within
cardboard. For moments,
you held in your palms
creation and creator
until it flew down to meet
its breaking, here,
in a home that still strives
to be home. But
what the cup held
the days of its holding
was meant to be turned
into a savouring,
a taste of solace
yet to come.

Offering

Kneeling by his grave, I offer my father
a cup of tea, the way he'd wanted it
before he died. I was eleven
when the rented wheelchair came.
I ploughed long furrows
into the carpets. He was home
after months in hospital.

Ringed by family, he asked for lemon tea—
a bit of sugar, not too hot.
Assigned the task, I went to the kitchen,
filled a mug with lukewarm water—
squeezed a tea bag against the side
to tint the water, a splash
of lemon from an ancient bottle.
Sugar—not enough. A precarious march
back to his bedside.

He sipped it and winced.
Good he said, though it wasn't.
Fell back to the pillow.

Christmas eve, he was wheeled out
for company. My mother, a red-eyed bullet
through the thrumming house.
Amid the clink of teacups,
he lay on the couch, filmed
with sweat from the toll
of being alive.

Quiet and cool in my room, I sat
alone with a box of Swiss chocolate,
miniatures in neat white cubicles.
The waxy sweetness
of the milk and white bars,
a prim smothering. The nuts
were grit on my teeth and tongue.
Only the bitter one tasted
of something I could have felt.

Today, at last, I've done it right.
A good pour of amber honey,
fresh lemon, boiling water, loose leaves—
tea brewed hot and strong.
Drink, my father, as I drink to you
this striving of sun, sky, earth and flesh
held within these porcelain cups.

Chrysanthemum Tea

As a child, I marvelled:
flowers I could drink.
Yellow granules in a yellow tin—
fragrance distilled for the tongue.
Pale gold elixir my mother dispensed
to quell a fever or aching throat.

Years later, I lift a teacup lid
to show my son the dried blossoms
blooming in a steaming collage
of leaves, crimson berries, rock sugar.
An undersea garden for the senses.
In the noodle house's clang and bustle,
we take little sips of grace.

Anniversary

In the shop, they're set apart
from the frowzy cheer
of sturdy potted mums.

Long-stemmed, long-petalled ones.
Clustered buds cocooned,
immaculate within their casings.

At the cemetery, I unwrap them
on the winter grass, placing them down
before those I've loved.

They open, like hands of gods,
a white multitude of fingers
unfurled— not to plead, but hold.

Poem

Like a small padded tree, you stood
with one hand outstretched, a red-mittened beacon.
The first scout whisked past. Soon, a flurry
perched on branches around us. At last,
a daring one hovered, darted to your palm
to snatch a seed, then fled. We both breathed again,
you crying out softly—
Here without seeds or words, I stand
before the fluttering world,
beckoning.

Transit

He slides his ticket
into the slot, pulls me past
steamed up windows to the rear.
We discuss emergency hatches,
plot escape scenarios. Tunnelling
through dark and rain,
my arms his seatbelts.
He tangles a leg with mine.

Passengers' heads like eggs
in a carton, sprawled
legs of teenaged boys.
Outside, the passing world—
seams of telephone and power lines,
worlds held within, beyond.

The bus heaves
to a stop. Disgorged,
we breathe, walk straight.

But soon enough,
we're aboard again—
another bus, route, day. Perpetual
arrival, departure. We traverse
the city's grid, marking
distance, marking time.

Kindergarten at the
Transylvania Flavour Restaurant

My son interrogates me.
A piece of schnitzel at lunch leads to
the location of Transylvania,
the origins of World Wars,
Pearl Harbour, and of course,
the Atomic bomb.
In fifteen minutes, breaded meat
leads to civilian massacre.
(Thank goodness for Sachertorte.)

I am a deficient encyclopedia.
I watch him savour his cake and recall
that Britannica set, twelve years out of date,
in its own special bookcase
that my mother bought for one hundred dollars.
Tiny lines of knowledge
on gold-edged pages bound
between heavy cream covers.

The atlas mapped our existence,
how far we'd come. A century per inch.
And then the clouds.

I always snuck off with the "anatomy" volume.
Human archaeology on transparent pages.
The skin of a naked Adam, a naked Eve.
Next, their striated muscles. The webs
of blood and nerve underneath, organs—

grey brain, pink lung, snaking
sausage of intestines—finally
the ultimate core of bone.
What I sought again and again.
How it happened that I am

Here. Eating schnitzel, cake,
with my son who came from my body
and his father's, through our ancestors' —
an Australian navigator routing his plane
to a dance in Winnipeg, a girl singing
her grief in a Saigon teahouse.
Learning, as my son is learning. Gathering
who we are, crumb by crumb.

Omelet

Some days, although we cannot pray, a prayer
utters itself....

—Carol Ann Duffy

First, the egg.
I teach him the way I taught myself,
food group by food group
through the tattered cookbook.
I break the eggs; he stirs them.
A flick of salt, a few drops of cream.
I heat the pan, grate the cheese.
He pours the eggs in. Opacity
spreads from the edges inward:
an ocean sizzles into land.
Perched on the countertop,
he observes me like the scientist
he might become.
I flip one side over. *Voila!*

Last night, we played a game
and pulled a card. What would the world
come to in a hundred years?
I feared a polluted war zone
unless humankind changed.
He said we'd live on Mars.

I pour the claret tea as fragrant
as a berry patch into the good cups.
Warming his hands, he wiggles his fingers

through the prospect of clouds.
He stirs in the honey, licks the spoon,
says *Thank you bees.*

White cyclamen on the table. Blaze of winter
sun through trees. A plate
of simple food. Beside us,
the ones we love.

Still, Life

No ladder, no kids to shake them down,
the high stubborn apples have gripped
the gnarled arms of their tree
after the descent of leaves, the last snowfall.
Still yellow, mere husks
sourly persisting as humans do.
Who do we wait for,
who awaits us?

Nascent leaves furled and tensed in their buds.
A few crocus tips in half-frozen soil.
How can these apples
imagine appleness now?

By the stove, a bowl of static apples
probably picked months ago, their ripening slowed
in the cool dark of shipping containers.
A *still life*, I tell my son, and point
at colour plates of Cezanne, Picasso.
The fruit does not move,
composed and stuck in some precise
slice of light and time.

He runs to the table to sketch out
the tree, the ground. Then the apples,
with new blue capes billowing out in the air.
They leap from their branches, never
falling, to their glorious fate.

Acknowledgements

I would like to thank the following anthologies, literary magazines and their poetry editors who have published or will be publishing some of the poems in this book in their earlier incarnations:

"Walking" in *The Antigonish Review*; "After the Party" in *Arborealis: A Canadian Anthology of Poetry*; "Park" broadcast on *North by Northwest* as part of the Fourth Annual CBC Poetry Face-Off, 2005; "Park" and "Beach" in *CV2*; "Naming" and "Father's Day" in *The Fiddlehead*; "Weed Killer" in *Grain*; "Chrysanthemum," "Before Breakfast" and "Home," in *The New Quarterly*; "Park," "Kindergarten at the Transylvania Flavour Restaurant," and "Dawn" in *Not a Muse: A World Anthology of Poetry*; "Mermaid", "Milk" and "Real" in *nthposition* online magazine; "Funeral March" as "Marche Funèbre" in *Other Voices*; "Glass" in *Our Times*; "Colic" in *Prairie Fire*; "Still, Life" and "Waiting" in *Prism International*; "Nursing Home" in *Room of One's Own*; and "Kite" in *A Verse Map of Vancouver*.

Epigraphs and extracts that appear in this collection are from the following books: "Winning" by Linda Gregg from *Things and Flesh* published by Graywolf Press in 1999; "On Angels" by Czeslaw Milosz from *Against Forgetting: Twentieth-Century Poetry of Witness* edited by Carolyn Forché and published by W. W. Norton in 1993; "Poem for a Daughter" by Anne Stevenson in *Selected Poems 1955–2005* published by Bloodaxe Books in 2005; "Prayer" by Carol Ann Duffy from *Mean Time* published by Anvil Press Poetry in 1993.

Two poet-mentors in particular were invaluable in preparing this collection of poems for publication: Anne Simpson for her generosity and expertise in getting under the skin of early drafts of the poems over the summer; and Barry Dempster through the Wired Writing Program at the Banff Centre for the Arts for performing the complex "heart surgery" necessary to complete and refine the manuscript. Thanks to the Wired Writing Program, Fred Stenson and the Banff Centre staff for providing the much needed time, space and support in the final sprint toward the finish line. My gratitude to Don Domanski for his sage advice about writing; to dear friend Susan Olding for her encouragement and support in generating new work; to Vici Johnstone at Caitlin Press and Marisa Alps at Harbour Publishing for their unwavering faith in my work and ceaseless efforts to promote local authors; and to Marty Gervais for his graciousness.

I am greatly indebted to my sister Shona Lam for her crucial ongoing assistance in every way, and to my brother Bruce Lam for his logistical support. Thank you to friends, helpers and colleagues: Vern Beamish, Oonagh Berry, Deborah Campbell, Shannon Cowan, Elizabeth Greene, Chris Hutchinson, Maureen Hynes, Dee Lanthier, Derry Lubell, Grace and Noralynn Mariano, Ellen McGinn, Krista Murray, Alex Pierce, Gary Ryder, Loretta Seto, Jane Hamilton Silcott, Lisa Stephenson, Cathy Stonehouse, Peter Tolliday and Analee Weinberger among many others. Most importantly, I thank my dearest Robbie and my deceased parents, Dr. Chung Nin Lam and Dr. Bik May Wai Lam, for their inspiration and love.

More fiction and poetry from Caitlin Press

A Well-Mannered Storm: The Glenn Gould Poems, Kate Braid
poetry,120 pp, pb, ISBN: 978-1-894759-28-1, $16.95

Lan(d)guage: A Sequence of Poetics, Ken Belford
poetry, 84 pp, pb, ISBN: 978-1-894759-29-8, $16.95

Pathways into the Mountains, Ken Belford
poetry, 94 pp, pb, ISBN: 978-0-920576-84-7, $14.95

Soft Geography, Gillian Wigmore
poetry, 80 pp, pb, ISBN: 978-1-894759-23-6, $15.95

All Things Said & Done, Marita Dachsel
poetry, 80 pp, pb, ISBN: 978-1-894759-22-9, $15.95

Finding Ft. George, Rob Budde
poetry, 128 pp, pb, ISBN: 978-1-894759-27-4, $15.95

A Northern Woman, Jaqueline Baldwin
poetry, 150 pp, pb, ISBN: 978-1-894759-01-4, $16.95

The Centre, Barry McKinnon
poetry, 104 pp, pb, ISBN: 0-920576-51-6, $12.95

The Last Three Hundred Miles, G. Stewart Nash
fiction, 168 pp, pb, ISBN: 978-0-920576-90-8, $18.95